P9-DBT-325

8-90

ARMSTRONG'S CHURCH OF GOD

BY
SALEM KIRBAN

DOCTRINES OF DEVILS
No. 1

Exposing the cults of our day

LIBRARY.
BRYAN COLLEGE
DAYTON, TN. 37321

MOODY PRESS
CHICAGO

53882

Copyright © 1970, 1973 by Salem Kirban
All rights reserved, including the right to reproduce
this book or portions thereof in any form.

Library of Congress Catalog Card No. 75-124142
MOODY PRESS EDITION, 1973
ISBN: 0-8024-0302-6

ACKNOWLEDGMENTS

To Dr. Gary G. Cohen, Professor of Greek and New Testament at Biblical School of Theology, Hatfield, Pennsylvania, who carefully checked the final manuscript and supplied the scripture references.

To Bob Krauss, artist, who skillfully did the finished art throughout the book.

Printed in the United States of America

ARMSTRONG'S
RADIO CHURCH OF GOD

A DIFFICULT TASK

"...no other work on earth is proclaiming this true Gospel of Christ to the whole world."

Herbert W. Armstrong

How does one write about a man he admires? I must admit I find it difficult...difficult because my findings must report that the Radio Church of God is a cult. And it departs from the Bible!

From the human standpoint, Herbert W. Armstrong is a tremendous personality, an excellent businessman. He has passed on these qualities to his son, Garner Ted Armstrong. And the two make an unbeatable team! Together they are "the work."

In my opinion the scope of their activities far outruns any single evangelical Christian organization or evangelist. If Herbert W. Armstrong were an evangelical Christian he would undoubtedly stand in the forefront as today's most valuable leader. For with his zeal, with his personal business "know-how" and with God's direction, I personally believe he would have the impact of two Dwight L. Moody's.

Within the framework of his own personal theology, Mr. Armstrong does not compromise. As an example, he would not have tolerated what was allowed at the recent Congress on Evangelism in Minneapolis when a group of hippies were given recognition and prominence.

Perhaps this can best be described by Herbert W. Armstrong's editorial in the February, 1970 issue of THE PLAIN TRUTH

3

where he discusses Ambassador College. Ambassador College in Pasadena, California, is one of three colleges founded by Armstrong.

> The *Los Angeles Times,* at the top of page 1 of a 640-page Sunday Edition, recently ran a story on a Utopian college campus. The word "utopia" was used in its headline. It was a story *The Times* did on a unique and different college campus, where there are no riots, there is no protest, there are no hippies, but where everybody is smiling and seems to be really happy!

I must be honest with you. I visited Ambassador College in Pasadena, California and was graciously given a tour of the entire Armstrong complex. From an earthly standpoint, it appears to be the closest thing to utopia that I have ever seen!

Humanly speaking, if I were not a Christian, I would quickly join Armstrong's Worldwide Church of God and attend his college. For it has everything this world has to offer.

And everything Herbert W. Armstrong does is TOP QUALITY! His methods of planning and promotion are without equal! And he is getting results.

But as a Christian, I cannot accept his theology. And as a Christian author, I must expose what I personally consider to be one of the most deadly cult forms existing today— The WORLDWIDE CHURCH of GOD... known by some as The RADIO CHURCH OF GOD, THE WORLD TOMORROW, THE PLAIN TRUTH or BRITISH ISRAELISM (ISRAELITISM).... or as ARMSTRONGISM!

Herbert W. Armstrong's brand of theology mixes a little truth with a little of his own theories. And if a Christian does not make a thorough study of this theology... he is bound to fall hook, line and sinker for THE PLAIN TRUTH message.

It is far easier for a Christian to discern the difference between Mormonism and Christianity or Buddhaism and Christianity... than to discern even that there is a vast, vast difference between Armstrong's WORLDWIDE CHURCH of GOD and Christianity! And this is where the danger lies!

Many Christians, in fact, will become highly insulted if one

4

even implies that Herbert W. Armstrong's message is contrary to God's Word. Several evangelical missionary directors have told me that some donors have cut off giving to an evangelical group when the director exposed Armstrong's misapplication of Bible truths!

Another reason I am writing this expose´ is because many who have read my other books (GUIDE TO SURVIVAL, 666, YOUR LAST GOODBYE) have questioned me about Herbert W. Armstrong's theology.

Armstrong must be challenged because, like all cults, ARM-STRONGISM never tires of casting reflections on anything that bears the name Christian. At the same time there is the constant implication given forth that Armstrong's church alone is "God's Church."

It is not a simple matter to pin down just what the Armstrongs believe. There is nothing like a creed in the Armstrong church. Christian terminology is used freely but with different meanings; and many people think Mr. Armstrong believes one thing when he doesn't believe anything of the kind. Simply, clearly, I hope this book conveys as accurately as possible both some of the things the Armstrongs believe and what the Bible tells us. I hope that in some measure to be forewarned is to be forearmed. In this way many can avoid falling victim to this cult.

As I said before, from a human standpoint, I admire Mr. Armstrong. How I pray that God will in these Last Days send men of his calibre— but true to the Word of God. We need such leadership.

Before we get to the heart of this treatise on the Worldwide Church of God...let me say one thing. Several articles have been written on Herbert W. Armstrong in derision. I do not intend to do this. I intend to show where Mr. Armstrong differs with Scrip-ture...but with Christian courtesy. It is also my praryer that God may yet lead Mr. Armstrong to a correct knowledge of His truth.

THE BITTER PILL

It was early March, 1970. I found myself driving from Los Angeles up the Pasadena Freeway headed for Ambassador College and Herbert W. Armstrong's Church of God headquarters. From the fast and furious pace of Los Angeles, when one turns off the Freeway into Pasadena you feel as though you are entering into a small country town.

Large, spacious homes, beautiful green lawns, wide streets with an aisle of green down the center...all this meets your eyes.

It was with keen anticipation that I looked forward to finally seeing first hand the work of a man I had heard so much about!

Suddenly, turning the corner, I looked...and there is was! It was like a utopia! Attractive grilled fencing surrounded Ambassador College. Magnificent, stately buildings, finely manicured lawns, and an inspiring spouting fountain.

And I wondered...how did this all start?

A DETERMINED WIFE

One might say that Mr. Armstrong's wife, Loma, was instrumental in forming his basic theories. This church...the official name of which is The WORLDWIDE CHURCH of GOD...emphasizes *legalism,*—similar to that advocated by the Seventh Day Adventists—but more on this will be said later.

Herbert W. Armstrong entered the business world in the field of advertising. And this fact alone has great bearing on his great success today. For he employs the very best techniques in advertising. And because he does, he is getting fantastic results.

Caught up in the depression years, he reports that three times his businesses were wiped out.

Perhaps this may have had some influence on him being "converted" by his wife. He had tried his own ways and they apparently failed.

In Herbert W. Armstrong's autobiography he tells of his wife's great discovery which was:

> ...obedience to God's spiritual laws summed up in the Ten Commandments is necessary for salvation.
>
> Not that our works of keeping the commandments save us, but rather that sin is the transgression of God's spiritual law. Christ does not save us in our sins but from our sins.
>
> We must repent of sin, repent of transgressing God's

6

law which means turning from disobedience as a prior condition to receiving God's gift. [1]

Mr. Armstrong initially was at odds with his wife's theories. In his early days he was what may be termed a nominal fundamentalist. Salvation to him was not by works...it was by grace.

But his wife would not give in. She firmly believed she was right...her husband wrong.

All these churches can't be wrong...he thought. And with determination he set out to prove his wife was wrong in her newfound theology. After much study especially of Seventh Day Adventist literature, and of literature of a Church of God with headquarters at Stanberry, Missouri, Armstrong came to the conclusion that "his wife had found the truth after all. It was a bitter pill to swallow." And as he relates..."a furious innerstruggle ensued within him."

Herbert W. Armstrong had swallowed the bitter pill...and the Radio Church of God was born, later to take the name of The Worldwide Church of God.

THE NEIGHBOR NEXT DOOR

In a sense you might say Herbert W. Armstrong's RADIO CHURCH OF GOD had its real beginnings with the neighbor next door to his parents.

For it was this neighbor who let Loma, his wife, in on the "great discovery" about the law of God. This neighbor was a member of the Church of God which was an offshoot of the Seventh-day Adventist Church. And much of today's Worldwide CHURCH OF GOD theology parallels this teaching such as:

1. The Seventh-day should be observed as the Sabbath
2. Abstinence from certain articles of food as unclean
3. Observance of the Old Testament feasts
4. Denunciation of the doctrine of eternal punishment in hell and advocating the annihilation of the wicked.
5. Extreme legalism

Shortly thereafter Mr. Armstrong was ordained by the Church

[1] The Autobiography of Herbert W. Armstrong, Ambassador College Press, 1967, Vol. 1, pp. 281 ff.

of God with headquarters in Stanberry, Missouri. Mr. Armstrong was not long content with their doctrinal beliefs and began submitting long articles embodying new doctrines. This very soon led to their refusal to support him and to his leaving them.

Some of these other new doctrines are:

6. Denial of the Trinity
7. Denial of the bodily resurrection of Christ
8. Belief that man may become God as God is God

At this point it may be wise to let Herbert W. Armstrong tell in his own words how this change in his theology came about. This excerpt appeared on page 6 of February 1970 issue of TOMORROW'S WORLD:

> ...when I was 34 years of age, my religious nonchalance was rudely jolted. My wife and I were visiting my parents in Salem, Oregon. Mrs. Armstrong returned from a visit with one of my mother's friends — a neighbor. This woman seemed to be a sort of "Bible Christian." She had handed her Bible to my wife and asked her to read a certain passage aloud. Then, without any comment whatever, she asked my wife to turn to another passage and read it aloud — then another and another. All these passages seemed to connect in an orderly sequence.
>
> "Why!" exclaimed my wife in astonishment, "this is not what I've always been taught! Have I always been led to believe *just the opposite* of what the Bible teaches?"
>
> "Well, don't ask me," smiled my mother's neighbor. "I didn't teach you a word. You just read it yourself out of the Bible."
>
> Mrs. Armstrong came running to tell me what she had discovered. Suddenly her religious belief had been changed. To me, she had become a religious fanatic. What she had read out of the Bible was diametrically contrary to the general teachings of the churches. I was angered, furious. Argument did no good. She had all the answers — and right out of the Bible. This was the incident that challenged and angered me into the first real study of the Bible of all my life.
>
> I said, "You can't tell me that all these churches are wrong. I know they get what they believe out of the Bible!" So I devoted six months to intensive, almost night and day, research and study to try to find, *in the Bible,* what I had been taught in church. I, too, was astounded to find just the opposite...

Focal point of lobby of Ambassador Hall is the beautiful fireplace with matching grained wood. Above fireplace is portrait of the late Loma D. Armstrong, wife of Herbert W. Armstrong. This majestic home was part of an estate of a millionaire. Ambassador College was founded by Mr. Armstrong in 1947.

It was a bitter decision — I now felt my life was worthless, but I told God that if He could use such a worthless life, I would give it to Him in unconditional surrender.

At last, once I swallowed my pride, admitted defeat, was humbled, had repented, and accepted the Christ of the Bible — a different Christ than I had previously pictured — I had found the true SOURCE for belief...

You know, sometimes I day dream...and in writing   s I was just wondering...what would have happened if that o\   zealous neighbor lady did not try to "evangelize" Mrs. Armstrong? Perhaps Herbert W. Armstrong in years to come would have found the true Gospel. Perhaps, too, he would have been one of today's moving forces for Christ in this world!

FINDING THE LOST TRIBES OF ISRAEL

Anglo-Israelism...sometimes called British-Israelism has existed in one way or another at least since the 18th Century.

Dr. Walter R. Martin, in his book THE KINGDOM OF THE CULTS, gives an excellent background on this belief. I recommend that you read it.

While Herbert W. Armstrong and his WORLD WIDE CHURCH OF GOD teach some of the doctrines of Anglo-Israelism...he goes even beyond this error into what I believe are other heretical teachings.

As Dr. Martin states: "The Radio Church of God (former name) is outside the historic Christian Church because it denies foundational Christian truth. Some other forms of Anglo-Israelism seem to endeavor to at least maintain a guarded orthodoxy in the areas of the Nature of God, personal redemption, and the Person and Work of Jesus Christ. THIS IS NOT THE SITUATION WITH ARMSTRONG'S GROUP..."

THE COUNTERFEIT CLAIM

British-Israelism is a *theory* that the Anglo-Saxon countries (Great Britain and its former empire plus the United States) are two of the 10 lost tribes of Israel, England being Ephraim and the United States being Manesseh, the two sons of Joseph. Other countries of northwestern Europe, such as northwestern France (Reuben) and Sweden are alleged to be the other tribes of Israel.

This theory is FALSE and without any Scriptural foundation!

Now from this initial premise that the British people are two of the Lost 10 Tribes of Israel the WORLDWIDE CHURCH OF GOD adds other equally false assumptions into its theology.

But first, let us examine the LOST TRIBE theory and see how this conclusion has been arrived at in the minds of those who adhere to it.

Herbert W. Armstrong's Views

ISRAEL and JUDAH *not* the same. In his article *WHERE ARE THE TEN LOST TRIBES?* Mr. Armstrong states:

We want to impress here that *Israel* and *Judah* are not two names for the same nation. They were and still are, and shall be until the Second Coming of Christ, two separate nations. The *House of Judah* always means *Jew*...

The next place where the term "Jew" is mentioned in the Bible, the *House of Israel* had been driven out in captivity, lost from view, and the term only applies to those of the *House of Judah.* There are no exceptions in the Bible.

What the Bible Says

"ISRAELITE" and "JEW" are used interchangeably by Apostolic Times (30-100 A.D.).

Judah, from which comes the term "Jew," was one of the 12 tribes of the nation Israel. In 931 B.C. the kingdom divided in two. The northern state with its 10 tribes took the name Israel while the southern state took the name Judah—for this tribe occupied almost all of its territory. In 722 B.C. Israel was conquered and scattered by Assyria and in 606 to 536 B.C. Judah went into captivity in Babylon. The conquests of both halves of the nation brought on a mixing of the two names. Thus these terms often were used interchangeably in Scriptures, and members of all 12 tribes came to be all called "Jews."

In the New Testament alone the word "Jew" is used 174 times and the term "Israel" 75 times. Impartial scholars agree these terms are often used interchangably.

PAUL THE APOSTLE *thusly uses the terms interchangeably...calling himself a "Jew" in Acts 21:39 and in 22;3 ... and an "Israelite" in Romans 11:1 (See these verses).*

What basically Mr. Armstrong is saying here is that the Jews of today come from only two of the 12 tribes of Israel, and that the other 10 are made up **today** of those in England (Ephraim), the United States (Manasseh), and those peoples of northwestern Europe. The true facts, however, are that those who are today called Jews are the descendants of all 12 of the tribes; and the British and American anglo-saxons (as fine as they may be) are not Ephraim or Manasseh.

Herbert W. Armstrong's Views	What the Bible Says

GOD'S COVENANT OF BLESSING belongs to Two Tribes, Ephraim and Manasseh

Those holding to the British-Israelism theory state that:

1. Jacob's two adopted sons, Ephraim and Manasseh are inheritors of the name of Israel.

2. God made an "unconditional and unbreakable" convenant with David. The Worldwide Church of God claims possession of a genealogy of this throne that goes clear back to Adam! Mr. Armstrong states:

   "The writer has a copy of this chart, and also his own genealogy for each generation back into the line of British kings and therefore has the complete record of his genealogy through the House of David clear to Adam — believe it or not!"[2]

3. Thus the House of Israel is not Jewish. Only those of the Tribe of Judah are the Jews. The House of Israel are the 10 lost tribes.

   Ephraim, one of the 10, then, is Great Britain. Manasseh, one of the 10, is the United States.

4. Thus the white English and white Americans, are heirs to all the promises that go with the Throne of David.

1. A careful reading of Ezekiel 37:15-17 will dispel Mr. Armstrong's theory that God's promises are primarily directed to only two tribes. Since Ephraim was both the centrally located and the strongest tribe of the Northern Kingdom of Israel, its name is used in Ezekiel 37:16 to represent the entire Northern Kingdom. But the words "his companions" refer to the other tribes of Israel.

2. It is today impossible for anyone to trace a genealogy all the way back to Adam. All the official Jewish records were destroyed with the destruction of the Temple by Titus in A.D. 70.

3. This belief is contrary to the Word of God. Such verses as Acts 21:39, 22:3 and 2 Corinthians 11:22 as well as Zechariah 8;13 confirm that the names Israel (Israelite) and Judah (Jew) are used for the identical people by the time of the Apostles.

4. Ezekiel 37:19-25 clearly shows God's promises are *both* to the tribes of the Northern Kingdom (Israel) *and* to Judah, the Southern Kingdom.

5. *If there is such a distinction between Israel and Judah, then how can the English and Americans—supposedly two tribes of Israel—claim David's throne when David was from Judah (Luke 3:31,33) and hence, a JEW???*

---

[2]The United States and British Commonwealth in Prophecy.

LANDMARKS (?)
AND
MANGLED HEBREW

It is the British-Israelism theory that the "lost" tribes left landmarks as they fled the Holy Land and migrated to the British Isles.

This group claims such superficial evidence as names of tribes which have been left behind in their trail.

1. They point out as an example:

The DANube River

and

DANzig

as clear indications to them of the trans-European migration of the Tribe of Dan.

They claim the term SAXON is derived from the Hebrew and means ISAAC-SON. Yet in Hebrew "Issac's Son" would be "Ben-Yitssac" or "Ben-Issac."

2. They state that the Hebrew term for COVENANT (berith or berit) and for MAN (ish) should be interpreted as "the man of the covenant."

Herbert W. Armstrong's reasoning goes like this:

A. The House of Israel is the COVENANT people;
The House of Israel is not Jewish!

B. The Hebrew word of COVENANT is *berith* or *berit*.
The Hebrew word for man is *ish*.

C. The Hebrew word for COVENANT is spelled in Hebrew *BRT*. Because vowels were generally not given in the spellings in original Hebrew... you have the Hebrew word for covenant. *BRT*, when Anglicized BRITH or BRIT.

Armstrong further states...

D. The Hebrews never pronounce their h's. So the Anglicized form of the Hebrew word for COVENANT is *BRIT*.

And now here is Mr. Armstrong's final analyzation:

E. If you take the word for COVENANT (BRIT) and the word for MAN (ISH)...the covenant people would therefore be BRIT-ISH. So the true covenant people today are called the British. And they reside in the British Isles....

3. To further prove his point, Mr. Armstrong states:

To Abraham God said, "In Isaac shall thy seed be called," and this name is repeated in Romans 9:7, Hebrews 11:18. In Amos 7:16 they are called the "house of Isaac."

Thus, it is Mr. Armstrong's belief that:

A. They are descended from Isaac, and therefore are Isaac's sons

B. Drop the "i" from Isaac (vowels are not generally used in Hebrew spelling) and you now have
Saac's sons

C. Or, as we have spelled it in shorter manner,
SAXONS

In effect, Mr. Armstrong has mangled Hebrew in order to justify his theory that England and the United States (the Anglo-Saxons) are the inheritor's of God's promise.

In reality, however, the Hebrew words *berith* and *ish,* are in the wrong order for his purpose. *Brit-ish* means "covenant of man," not, "man of the covenant" which would be ISH-BRIT.

TRANSPORTING THE THRONE

Furthermore the Worldwide Church of God maintains that the throne of England is the throne of David!

In the June, 1953 issue of THE PLAIN TRUTH appears the following statement:

...Elizabeth II actually sits on the throne of King David of ISRAEL—that she is a direct descendent, continuing David's dynasty—the VERY THRONE on which Christ shall sit after His return...

Mr. Armstrong is misled on the continuing THRONE OF DAVID. In 2 Samuel 7:13 we read, "He shall build an house for my name, and I will establish the throne of his kingdom forever." This "forever" did NOT mean that the Throne of

BRITAIN'S CORONATION CHAIR

What today appears to be merely an "ancient relic" in reality represents the throne of David. Not this literal 1296 A.D. oak chair, but the stone over which it is built, the "pillow stone" of Jacob, the stone that was "overturned, overturned, overturned" (Ezekiel 21:27) and will be moved only once more when Christ comes to claim David's throne.

Keystone Photo

Photographically reproduced from page 21 of May-June, 1970 issue of TOMORROW'S WORLD.

David would be in continuous uninter..pted existence here on earth. But Mr. Armstrong thinks otherwise. I'. states:

> ...The Throne of David, occupied by Solomon, was to be established FOR EVER! If that throne ever ceased to exist, then God's promise has failed!...
>
> If the throne of David ceased with Zedekiah, then it does not exist today, *how shall Christ sit upon a non existent throne?*[3]

If I interpret Mr. Armstrong's position correctly the "forever" in the verse above would imply for him that the Throne of David must be in continuous existence here on earth. And if it did not...God's promise has failed.

That would be his position. Without getting overly into detail here...this analysis is further carried down to show that Great Britain and the United States are the inheritors of God's promises and that Queen Elizabeth is in actuality sitting on the Throne of David.

This succession of events works out well for the proponents of British-Israelism and the Worldwide Church of God. Unfortunately, while it sounds very logical to some, it is just NOT Scriptural.

Scripture tells us:

> 1. The Throne of David ceased for the time being—until Christ returns—with Zedekiah. Zedekiah was the last king of the Southern Kingdom. During the final deportation of Jews to Babylon the Chaldeans overtook Zedekiah and carried him, the last king of Judah, to Babylon. See 2 Kings 25:7.
>
> 2. God delivered the Northern Kingdom of Israel into the hands of the Assyrians because of the wickedness of King Hoshea. This happened in 721 B.C.

If Mr. Armstrong holds to his theory that since that time the Throne of David was in continuous existence...then he is at odds with Acts 15:12-18 which tells us that the "tabernacle" or House of David is fallen down. And also Amos 9:11 which prophecies that the tabernacle of David *will remain a ruins* until God has taken out of the Gentiles a people for His name in the Last Days.

[3]The United States and British Commonwealth in Prophecy.

16

A few of the many books offered to readers of THE PLAIN TRUTH and TOMORROW'S WORLD as well as radio and telecast viewers.

Hosea 3:4,5, however, tells us that the Throne of David will *not* be in continuous existence...that the children of Israel shall "abide many days without a king," and the Throne shall not return until the Jews "seek the Lord their God and David their king." Then, at that future time, God will establish the Throne of David forever.

While it would be advantageous for Mr. Armstrong port this Throne of David to England...it is not Script

> And so all Israel shall be saved: as it is written, There shall come out of Sion the Deliverer, and shall turn away ungodliness from Jacob...   (Romans 11:26)

> HERE AGAIN NOTE THIS CONFUSION: Armstrong claims that the British nations are the TRUE ISRAEL and hence the Throne of David belongs to them—to Queen Elizabeth today.

> SCRIPTURE, HOWEVER, is absolutely clear that David was from the Tribe of JUDAH (Jew) and that Jesus Christ, the Saviour, will someday forever occupy the Throne of David (Isa, 9:7)—and he too was from JUDAH (Jew)! Revelation 5:5.

> DO YOU SEE? Even if the British were one of the 10 tribes of Israel (Ephraim)—which they are positively not—the Throne of David would still not belong to them (Ephraim) because God has forever put it in the hands of the tribe of JUDAH (Jew)! And Christ, of Judah, shall reign upon it (Revelation 5:5; Isaiah 9:7).

ROBBERS OF THE PROMISE

What in effect does this British-Israelism theory do to God's promises?

1. It turns the study of prophecy into a topsy-turvy mystery wherein Israel refers to the modern English people. Thus, according to British Israelism, Jeremiah 23:7-8 teaches us that the English and American (English descent) peoples will eventually be gathered by God back to Palestine.

2. It exalts England and the United States (fine as they might or might not be) as Abraham's children, when they have no credible historical geneological link with Abraham.

3. It robs the Jewish nation, the true Israel, of many promises. By transferring God's promises from the Jewish nation such a

attention from the Jews...and tries to apply these
of God instead to Anglo-saxons. Thus Romans 11:1,
ger looks forward to the eventual conversion and
n of the Jews, but to the *conversion and restoration*
the Jews AND the Anglo Saxons!

THE 19-YEAR TIME CYCLES

W. Armstrong believes that he has a divine mandate
and one of his publications states:

> Yet He (Christ) had foretold a prophecy. He had foretold
> wolves coming in sheep's clothing to deceive the world. He
> had said they would enter in professing to come in His
> name claiming to be Christian, yet deceiving the whole
> world. That happened! [4]

Mr. Armstrong believes the whole world is religiously deceived. And by his statement that "...no other work on earth is
proclaiming this true Gospel of Christ to the whole world" he
by implication indicts evangelical churches as wolves coming
in sheep's clothing to deceive the world. In his view, this
"deception" would be because fundamentalists claim the
promises of God refer to Israel...not to Great Britain and the
United States; that salvation is by faith and the wicked shall
suffer eternally in hell. These are a few of the areas evangelical
Christians would differ with Mr. Armstrong.

Mr. Armstrong believes further that:

> 1. For two 19-year cycles the original apostles proclaimed
> the Gospel but that in A.D. 69—they fled.
>
> 2. In A.D. 70 Jerusalem was under a military siege. And
> for 18 1/2 centuries the Gospel was not preached! The
> world was deceived into accepting a false gospel.
>
> 3. Then Christ raised up His work and once again allotted
> two 19-year time cycles for proclaiming His same Gospel,
> preparatory to His Second Coming. THE WORLD TO-
> MORROW (radio & TV) and THE PLAIN TRUTH (maga-
> zine) are Christ's instruments which He is powerfully
> using....Once again it is the voice in the wilderness of
> religious confusion. [4]

After reading Mr. Armstrong's explanation of his divine
mandate in carrying out two more 19-year cycles...is it no

[4] The Inside Story of the World Tomorrow Broadcast, pages 7-11.

wonder that many become confused!

If we are to follow Mr. Armstrong's words...then
1. His first 19-year cycle began in January,
THE PLAIN TRUTH magazine began.

This first cycle then ended in January of 1953.

2. His second 19-year cycle began in January,
should end in January 1972.

Since I am writing this in 1970...2 years before the e. Mr.
Armstrong's second 19-year cycle, then "His Second
Coming" is to take place in January 1972. Obviously Mr.
Armstrong will have to explain how he can point with certainty to
the time of Christ's Second Coming when Scripture tells us that
the time of this event is completely hidden from us (Matt. 24:42-
44).

**(The above paragraph was written in our first edition and now, at this
later date, February 1973, it speaks for itself!)**

If one is to be true to the Scriptures then one must arrive at the
conclusion that the wolves coming in sheep's clothing are NOT
evangelical Christians...but rather those who hold to the belief of
British-Israelism and the Worldwide Church of God.

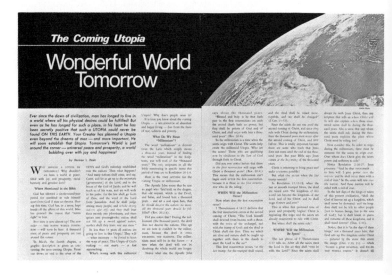

*May-June, 1970 issue of TOMORROW'S WORLD which states that
Millennium will occur in less than 15 years.*

cult diverts
promises
26 no l
oratio
of .

1932 and

nd of

Ambassador College new HALL OF ADMINISTRATION. Located here are most of the top executive offices for the worldwide educational program.

GARNER TED ARMSTRONG PLANS
NATIONWIDE SERIES OF PERSONAL APPEARANCES

On June 20, 1970, "the Work" (as Herbert W. Armstrong calls it) inaugurated a new thrust — "a *decisive* thrust which will soon catapult the Work into national and international prominence." [1]

On that Saturday night and also on Sunday, Monday and Tuesday, Garner Ted Armstrong began a series of personal appearances in Nashville, Tennessee.

After Nashville, Garner Ted Armstrong went to Cincinnati. And plans are to go to other cities "until *all* America gets the message."

Announcement of this new thrust was made in the May-June, 1970 issue of TOMORROW'S WORLD, in a three-page article titled FACE TO FACE WITH THE NATION. See below.

The article states:

> The program will be stimulating, educational, entertaining, and inspiring. The theme will be our great country — our heritage — our God — our blessed land — and the United States of America...The Ambassador College Chorale and Swingphonic Band — from both our Pasadena and Texas campuses — will perform...

> Questions will be welcome...the planning...directly under the immediate supervision of Mr. Ted Armstrong and the

overall supervision of Mr. Herbert Armstrong...

There will be no admission charge whatsoever...neither will any pseudosanctimonious "pitch" be made...

The article closes by reminding the Co- Workers to "produce — and give — and sacrifice — as we never have before.

[1] TOMORROW'S WORLD, May-June 1970, pages 24,25,26

ARMSTRONG PUBLICATION CLAIMS MILLENNIUM WILL BEGIN IN LESS THAN 15 YEARS

On page 18 of the May-June, 1970 issue of TOMORROW'S WORLD appears a five-page article titled *The Coming Utopia...WONDERFUL WORLD TOMORROW.*

Written by Herman L. Hoeh, Senior Editor, the article reports:

God has allowed a six-thousand-year period for mankind to rule himself apart from God if man so chooses. During this time, God has, in a sense, kept hands off the affairs of this world...

But time is now almost up! The new order — THE HAPPY WORLD TOMORROW — will soon be here. A thousand years of peace and prosperity are just around the corner...

In less than 15 years all nations are going to live in this Utopia!

...It is time you knew about the coming Utopia — a MILLENNIUM of abundant and happy living...

Further in this article the author agrees that the thousand year Millennium must occur *after* the second coming of Christ, and NOT before.

In light of this one wonders how he can place a date as to the coming of the Millennium ("in less than 15 years") when the Tribulation Period must precede the Millennium.

And perhaps more important is the fact that nowhere in God's Word does He tell us the exact date in which He will return at His second coming.

"Watch therefore: for ye know not what hour your Lord doth come...

Therefore be ye also ready: for in such an hour as ye think not the Son of man cometh."

(Matthew 24:42,44)

23

ARMSTRONG on the TRINITY

The *purpose of life is that in us* God is really re-creating his *own kind—reproducing himself* after his own kind...we grow spiritually more and more like God, until, at the time of the resurrections we shall be instantaneously *changed* from mortal into *immortal*—we shall then be *born of God—We shall then be God!* [5]

...I suppose most people think of God as one single individual Person. Or, as a *"trinity," This is not true.*

...the theologians...have blindly accepted the false doctrine introduced by *pagan* false prophets who crept in, that the Holy Spirit is a third person—the heresy of the *"trinity."* This *limits* God to "Three Persons." [6]

THE BIBLE ON THE TRINITY

No, the Bible is the book that teaches us of the TRI-UNITY (Trinity). The Bible tells us that there is but *one* God (Deut. 6:4—UNITY). It, however, also discloses that there are three divine persons (TRI) in this one Godhead.

The Bible shows us that each one in the Godhead is a PERSON—with the attributes of a person: self-consciousness, feelings, emotions, etc. (Thus Eph. 4:30 commands us not to "grieve"—make sad—the Holy Spirit. The Holy Spirit is called by a name, "The Comforter"—John 16:7. The Holy Spirit can be sinned against—Matt. 12:31).

The Bible shows us that each person in the Godhead is DIVINE—thus Jesus manifests omniscience in John 1:47-51 and makes divine claims in Revelation 1:8, 11, 22:13.

The Scriptures further associate all three of these together giving us the further impression of the truth of the Trinity (Tri-unity). Matt. 28:19; Luke 3:21-22, here the Father's voice is heard, the Spirit descends, and the Son is present bodily. Note also that in the Book of Revelation that the Dragon, the Beast, and the False Prophet comprise a False Trinity which seeks to duplicate the TRUE. Revelation 19:20; 13:4.

[5] Why Were You Born? pages 21, 22.
[6] Just What Do You Mean—Born Again? pages 17, 19.

ARMSTRONG ON CHRIST

Jesus *alone* of all humans, has so far been saved!

He was the first human ever to achieve it—to be perfected, finished as a *perfect character.* [7]

The Satan-inspired doctrine that Jesus was *not* human, that He did *not* inherit the human nature of Adam, that He did *not* have all the normal human nature of Adam, that He did *not* have all the normal human passions and weaknesses against which all of us have to struggle—in a word, that Jesus did *not* really come "in the flesh" as a normal human being—*This is the doctrine of the anti-Christ.*

The *only difference* between Jesus and any other humans is that He was conceived of the Holy Spirit. Therefore He obeyed God's laws *from birth...* [8]

THE BIBLE ON CHRIST

Jesus *alone* was born sinless and he lived a sinless life (John 8:46). Jesus, therefore, alone never needed to be saved and never was saved.

Jesus indeed was human, and the true humanity of Christ has been affirmed by orthodox christians throughout the centuries. He tired as did a true human; he thirsted; he was born and he died. He was human—but yet without sin (Heb. 4:15).

The Scriptures teach that the eternal divine Son, the Word (John 1:1,14), became flesh. That is, the second person of the trinity was born—and he was *one person* with two natures, the human and the divine. He was truly God and truly man; nevertheless, he was one person, the man Christ Jesus.

This divine-human Christ died and this same Christ was raised from the dead in the same body in which he was crucified (Romans 6:9-10; Luke 24:39; John 20:27). The Scriptures affirm that Christ died and that he now lives. They, nor the orthodox churches through the centuries, never split up the death between the body and the spirit—which Armstrong argues about. No, the whole divine-man Christ died for our sins, and this same divine man was resurrected. This is the teaching of Scripture whether or not Mr. Armstrong feels that it is rational or not.

---

[7] Why Were You Born? pages 11, 14.
[8] The PLAIN TRUTH, Vol. 28, No. 11, November, 1963.

ARMSTRONG ON RESURRECTION OF CHRIST

...God the Father did not cause Jesus Christ to get back into the body which had died.

Some seem to believe that it was only the *body* which died—that Jesus Christ never died.

What they believe is that a *body* Christ lived and died, but Christ *Himself* never died. Christ was God, and they argue, God could not die!

If Christ did not die for their sins—if it was only a mortal *body which* died, then we have no Saviour, and we are *lost.*

Jesus Christ was *dead*...And the resurrected body was no longer human—it was the Christ resurrected, *immortal,* once again changed! [9]

(Christ's)...resurrected body was no longer human.

Now notice carefully God the Father did not cause Jesus Christ to get back into the body which had died. Nowhere does the Scripture say He was alive and active or that God had Him get back into the human body that had died and was now resurrected...and the resurrected body was no longer human...He was changed and converted into immortality...

THE BIBLE ON THE RESURRECTION OF CHRIST

John 2:19-21 states: "Jesus answered and said unto them, Destroy this temple, and in three days I will raise it up.

Then said the Jews, Forty and six years was this temple in building, and wilt thou rear it up in three days?

But He spake of the temple of his body."

After the resurrection of Christ Luke 24:37-39 states:

"But they were terrified and affrighted, and supposed that they had seen a spirit.

And He said unto them, Why are ye troubled? and why do thoughts arise in your hearts?

Behold my hands and my feet, that is I myself: [Note that the resurrected Jesus is in the same body in which he died] handle me, and see; for a spirit hath not flesh and bones, as ye see me have."

And in John 20:24-29 even Thomas could not doubt that Christ had risen in physical form. As the Scriptures point out, Christ conquered death *as a whole man; not* as a mere spirit.

We are further told that at the Second Coming of Christ, when the dead in Christ rise, they will rise immortal and will possess a form like Christ's own form (I John 3:2).

---

[9] The PLAIN TRUTH, April, 1963, page 10.

26

Outgoing mail — bags of PLAIN TRUTHS, Pasadena plant. Upwards of TWO MILLION copies (soon to exceed that) represents a huge mailing. *The* PLAIN TRUTH is one of the major mass-circulation magazines in the world today.

UNEXPECTED DEMAND FOR MAGAZINES
CAUSES CURTAILMENT OF MONTHLY PUBLICATION

In both TOMORROW'S WORLD[1] and The PLAIN TRUTH[2], Herbert W. Armstrong made the following important announcement. We reprint excerpts from this announcement:

For the next six months, TOMORROW'S WORLD and The PLAIN TRUTH will be issued bimonthly [every two months]*.
Important developments have led to this temporary change.

It is due largely to unexpected and unprecedented GROWTH in the circulation of these magazines. This very success evidences the fact that people worldwide are HUNGRY for the priceless things we are able to give. This is fulfilling the GREATEST NEED in the world today!...

In the United States we purchased full-page advertising space in LIFE...in LOOK...in many issues of TV GUIDE... Our ads offered trial subscriptions to The PLAIN TRUTH. Also we purchased two-page space for the same ads in READER'S DIGEST in many foreign editions around the world...

The response was OVERWHELMING—far in excess of expectations. At the end of the three months' trial subscription, these subscribers were offered a year's already paid subscription. An astonishingly high percentage renewed for the full year's subscription...

But all this overwhelming response did TWO THINGS:

1. It shot The PLAIN TRUTH circulation from a little over one million to more than TWO MILLION COPIES.

2. This sudden jump in circulation of The PLAIN TRUTH forced us to buy additional huge 4-color web-fed magazine presses—build larger printing plants—increase number of employees in these plants—increase numbers of personnel on staffs in offices around the world...

RESULT? We had to build an entirely NEW printing plant in England, and in Pasadena, and also move our presses into larger quarters in North Sydney. But these plants *already are outgrown!* So both in Pasadena and at Radlett, England, we are proceeding to DOUBLE the size of these plants...

This great Work is financed by the contributions of 125,000 Co-Workers who BELIEVE in this vital program leading hundreds of thousands into a BETTER QUALITY LIFE! Although we DO NOT SOLICIT NEW CONTRIBUTORS all have become contributors VOLUNTARILY and without solicitation or urging by us—nevertheless, it is necessary to EXPLAIN that there is *need,* under present circumstances to increase revenues.

The very GROWTH and SUCCESS of our circulation-expansion program has increased operational expenditures. Therefore it is incumbent on me to make a frank and candid STATEMENT to our readers of the ENTIRE circumstances that have led to the *temporary* bi-monthly policy for The PLAIN TRUTH. This is not a request—we want new Co-Workers to *become* contributors voluntarily—unsolicited. But when additional ones do wish to have part in this great Work, in *whatever* amount, they are welcomed gratefully...

[1]TOMORROW'S WORLD, March-April 1970, pages 3, 4 and 34.
[2]The PLAIN TRUTH, April-May, 1970, pages 1 and 48.
*Both these magazines were previously printed *monthly.*

ARMSTRONG on SALVATION

Salvation...is a *process!*

But how the god of this world would blind your eyes to that! He tries to deceive you into thinking all there is to it is just "accepting Christ" with "no works" — and presto-chango, you are pronounced "Saved."

But the *Bible* reveals that *none* is yet 'saved.'[10]

People have been taught, falsely, that "Christ *completed* the plan of salvation on the Cross" — when actually it was only *begun* there.

The popular denominations have taught, "Just believe — that's all there is to it; believe on the Lord Jesus Christ, and you are that instant *saved!*"

That teaching is false! And because of deception — because the *true Gospel* of Jesus Christ has been blotted out, lo these 1900 years by the preaching of a false gospel *about the person* of Christ — and often a false Christ at that — millions today *worship* Christ — and all in vain!

The *blood* of Christ does not finally save any man.

The death of Christ merely paid the penalty of sin in our stead — it wipes the slate clean of our past sins — it saves us merely from the *death penalty...*

But we are *saved* — that is, given immortal life —by Christ's *life,* not by His death...

It is *only those* who, during this Christian, Spirit-begotten life,

    (A)   have grown in knowledge and grace

10 Why Were You Born? page 11

THE BIBLE on SALVATION

Process or instantaneous? Let us clarify this by examining "sanctification," God's making us holy. Sanctification is divided into three spheres by theologians:

(1) Initial sanctification (SALVATION)—Here God legally *declares* the wicked sinner who believes on Christ to be saved, justified. This is instantaneous—believe (repent and trust) and you are saved! Acts 16:31.

(2) Subjective sanctification—God's spirit DAILY CLEANSING the saved person from sins which would hinder your fellowship with God. I John 1:9.

(3) Final sanctification—Called "GLORIFICATION." This is God's finally making the believer perfect at the Second Coming of Christ or at our going to be with the Lord (Rom. 8:30; I Cor. 15:52-53).

Thus Armstrong confuses Initial Salvation, Subjective Sanctification (DAILY CLEANSING), and Final Glorification.

Mr. Armstrong believes that the new birth is divided into two segments —first a "beggeting" or conception upon acceptance of Christ and then the new birth (born again) itself at the resurrection of the body.

This is not Scriptural for I Peter 1:23 refers to our being born again in the past tense —not the future tense.

Dr. Walter R. Martin points out that the Greek rendition of Ephesians 2:8 reads: "By grace you have been saved through faith; and this is not your own doing, it is the gift of God — not

ARMSTRONG on SALVATION	THE BIBLE on SALVATION

ARMSTRONG on SALVATION

    (B)   have overcome
    (C)   have developed spiritually
    (D)   done the works of Christ
    (E)   and endured unto the end
who shall finally be given *immortality* — finally changed from mortal to *immortal* at the time of the Second Coming of Christ. [11]

...it is not only possible but *obligatory* that we obey God's spiritual law, the *ten commandments,* as they are magnified throughout the Bible. [12]

The *Bible,* which is God's *message* and *instruction to mankind,* nowhere teaches any such thing as the *pagan* doctrine of an "immortal soul" going to heaven at death. It teaches that the soul is *mortal,* and shall *die...*[13]

THE BIBLE on SALVATION

because of works, lest any one should boast."

Other supporting passages of Scripture include:

John 5:24; 6:47; Romans 8:1; I Peter 1:18; I John 5:1, 11-13, 20.

The Bibles portrays salvation as is an instantaneous event made possible by the grace of God (Acts 16:31; 2:8-10; Colossians 1:13, 14; Galatians 2:20, and 2 Corinthians 5:17).

Basically, Armstrong's brand of salvation is based on something that is GOING to happen. The Bible tells us that salvation is made available to us on the basis of something that HAS ALREADY HAPPENED! See I Corinthians 15:1-4; Hebrews 1:3,9:26, 28.

In answer to Mr. Armstrong's shocking statement that "the *blood* of Christ does not finally save any man" read I Peter 1:18, 19. Note that this verse is in the *past tense.*

Mr. Armstrong's great attachment of "keeping the law and commandment of God" as necessary parts of salvation is reminiscent of the Epistle to the Galatians where Paul scathingly denounced this as a heresy.

"Knowing that a man is not justified by the works of the law, but by the faith of Jesus Christ..." *THAT IS, Paul's letter to the Galatians was written to teach them that they are heretics who teach that in order to be saved one must do works and obey laws in addition to believing. This is precisely the Armstrong error.*

11 All About Water Baptism, pages 1, 2, 3, 8
12 The Plain Truth Magazine, November, 1963, pages 11, 12
13 Just What Do You Mean Born Again? pages 13, 14

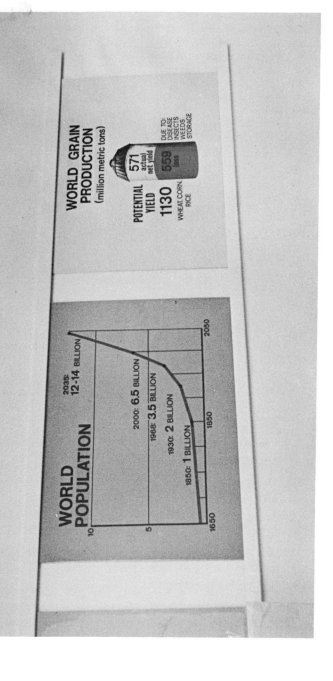

WORLD GRAIN
PRODUCTION
(million metric tons)

POTENTIAL
YIELD
1130
WHEAT, CORN,
RICE

571
actual
net yield

559
loss

DUE TO:
DISEASE
INSECTS
WEEDS
STORAGE

WORLD
POPULATION

10

5

2035:
12-14 BILLION

2000: 6.5 BILLION

1968: 3.5 BILLION

1930: 2 BILLION

1850: 1 BILLION

1650   1850   2050

Ambassador College Press maintains a top quality art department producing highly informative statistical charts both for their magazines and telecasts.

THE BIBLE on SALVATION

I do not frustrate the grace of God for if righteousness come by the law, then Christ is dead in vain.

(Galatians 2:21)

...no man is justified by the law in the sight of God...The just shall live by faith. And the law is not of faith...Christ hath redeemed us from the curse of the law."

(Galatians 3:11-13)

"...there be some that trouble you, and would pervert the Gospel of Christ.

But though we, or an angel from heaven, preach any other Gospel unto you than that which we have preached unto you, let him be accursed." (Galatians 1:8)

BUILDING A HEAVEN ON EARTH

In his book, THE KINGDOM OF THE CULTS, Dr. Walter R. Martin accurately describes the situation when he states:

> ...the theology of Herbert Armstrong and his Radio Church of God contains just enough truth to make it attractive to the listener who is unaware of the multiple sources of heretical doctrine he has drawn upon...enough of which permeates both his radio programs and his publications to insure the uninformed listener a gospel of confusion unparalleled in the history of American cultism....

The most dangerous aspect is that the Worldwide Church of God makes profuse use of the Bible while, in reality, its sole allegiance is to the interpretations of the Scripture propagated by Herbert W. Armstrong.

And his Worldwide Church of God will have even greater impact in future days...sidetracking Christians and the Lord's money because they cannot discern the difference!

From a human standpoint, Herbert W. Armstrong and the *WORLDWIDE CHURCH OF GOD are highly successful. Let's look at the record:*

COMPARATIVE

CHARTS

on the

12 TRIBES OF ISRAEL

THE BIBLE

vs.

ARMSTRONG'S THEORY

Published by SALEM KIRBAN Inc., Kent Road, Huntingdon Valley, Penna. 19006. Copyright © 1970 by Salem Kirban. Printed in the United States of America. All rights reserved, including the right to reproduce this book or portions thereof in any form.

Library of Congress Catalog Card No. 75-124142

HOW THE 12 TRIBES OF ISRAEL ORIGINATED

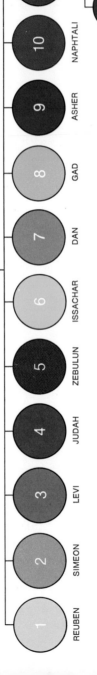

Jacob had 12 sons by four mothers: Leah, Rachel, Bilhah and Zilpah.

JACOB

| 1 REUBEN | 2 SIMEON | 3 LEVI | 4 JUDAH | 5 ZEBULUN | 6 ISSACHAR | 7 DAN | 8 GAD | 9 ASHER | 10 NAPHTALI | 11 JOSEPH | 12 BENJAMIN |

JOSEPH — MANASSEH, EPHRAIM — 2 SONS *

Jacob lived with Joseph in Egypt the last 17 years of his life. Before he died, he placed Joseph's two sons, Manasseh and Ephraim, on the same level as his own sons. See Genesis 48:5, 13-22. Also read the entire 48th Chapter of Genesis.

Now 13, not 12, Tribes came into being since Joseph's Tribe was divided into two Tribes (Manasseh and Ephraim).

HOWEVER, in the distribution of the Land made by Joshua, the Tribe of LEVI had *no share* in the Land (Joshua 13:14), but only cities scattered throughout Israel to dwell in and pasture land for their cattle (Joshua 14:4). Thus God, by dividing Levi among the others, retained the number of land holding tribes at 12, the original number of Jacob's sons.

The LEVITES (Tribe of LEVI) had no inheritance in Israel; the Lord was their inheritance. See Deuteronomy 10:9.

In the MARCHES of the ARMY of Israel The LEVITES performed the priestly functions (Deuteronomy 33:10), marching behind the second echelon of Tribes (Numbers 2:17).

Levites marched with Ark of the Lord

Ambassador College campus in Pasadena, California is filled with many picturesque scenes. This stream was built in 1959 by students then in College. In the background is a view of Mayfair, one of the many beautiful student residences. Ambassador College also has a campus in Texas and one some five miles from the outskirts of London, England.

THE PLAIN TRUTH is a magazine Mr. Armstrong began in 1934. In January, 1960, the circulation of THE PLAIN TRUTH was about 210,000 copies.

Today, 1973, the circulation is more than 2,500,000 copies — more than TEN TIMES the circulation of ten years ago! Think of it — 2½ MILLION COPIES distributed *every month!*

In January, 1960 THE PLAIN TRUTH was a 32-page two-color magazine. Today, 1973, it is a 52-page FULL-color magazine. Its quality equals any publication printed!

In January, 1960, only four names were listed on the staff. Today, 1973, THE PLAIN TRUTH has 65 names on its editorial staff.

This does not include the hundreds of employees in three large printing plants in Pasadena, California, in Radlett, England, and North Sydney, Australia!

THE PLAIN TRUTH is now published in five languages.

In 1969 another magazine by Herbert W. Armstrong flooded the market. It's name...TOMORROW'S WORLD.

TOMORROW'S WORLD was published by the Graduate School of Theology of Armstrong's AMBASSADOR COLLEGE. It purported to cover the field of Biblical understanding.

Started in 1969 the circulation of TOMORROW'S WORLD grew to 811,000, when for economy reasons, it was discontinued in April, 1972.

Herbert W. Armstrong makes a strong emphasis on *tithing*.

The January, 1970 issue of TOMORROW'S WORLD has six pages devoted to an article by a contributing editor, Leslie L. McCullough, titled THY KINGDOM COME!

In this article much emphasis is placed on GOD'S KINGDOM HERE ON EARTH.

In a section headed:
What Is God's Kingdom Anyway?
the author reflects:

The religions of this world softly drool about the "Gospel of Jesus." But what they don't teach — and probably don't know — is that the "Gospel" is simply the *advance news* of the Kingdom of God...

Then he goes on to say:

Over TWO MILLION copies of each issue of The PLAIN TRUTH are mailed. It represents one of the major mass-circulation magazines in the world today.

In one sentence, the Kingdom of God is the Government of Almighty God ruling over the entire earth.

At the end of this article the author continues:

But the question is: How will you respond? Even God doesn't know. He's anxiously awaiting your decision! Will your Creator be able to use you? Or will He be forced to call someone else to take your place?

You have been offered an awesomely stunning opportunity to participate in God's Word and to help save this world. And, as a bonus for your selfless humanitarianism, God will give you the gift of *Eternal Life* and the exalted position of a Ruling Son in His Royal Family.

But there are responsibilities. Here's what you *must* do! You must be totally engrossed in God's Work!

That means enthusiastically devoting *much* of your *prayers* to God's Work.

As many thousands of TOMORROW'S WORLD subscribers who are Co-Workers with Christ in this great Work realize, it also means cheerfully sending God's *tithes* and *offerings* to His Work!

No one who selfishly prays about himself all the time and no one who covetously lavishes all of his money on himself will ever gain eternal life. *Your personal salvation is directly related to how immersed you become in the Work of Almighty God.* [*NOTE THIS LEGALISM!*]

And the February, 1970 issue of TOMORROW'S WORLD has almost 4 pages on the subject titled: TITHING PAYS HERE'S THE PROOF!

Initially the article on the first two pages (pages 30 and 31) explain the Scriptures and tithing. It is not until the third column on page 32 that the reader is cleverly drawn into the real purpose of the article.

The paragraph head reads:

Where Should You Send God's Tithes?

After giving excerpts from letters from readers who showed how they were rewarded after sending their tithes to the Radio Church of God...the following letter is printed:

"After much fighting with my conscience I now believe in my heart I have been cheating God, but there is one thing that I need help on. I do not belong to a church. So where can I send God's money? Could you please tell me where to send God's money?"

The Senior Editor of TOMORROW'S WORLD, Roderick C. Meredith, then devotes more than a column directing the reader to send God's tithe to "His true representatives!"

Some of the excerpts from this column then go on to say:

> Somewhere on earth today are the true ministers of God...

> You had better check up and PROVE to yourself that The WORLD TOMORROW broadcast is the Work on earth which is fulfilling Christ's commission! If this is not yet clear to you, then just keep an open mind and let the fruits PROVE to you where Almighty God is really working!

> Check up and see where the truth of the Bible is being made PLAIN and CLEAR. Determine *positively* for yourself (Acts 17:11) where the *real* Good News of the Kingdom of God (TOMORROW'S WORLD) is being preached! (Matt. 24:14)

In reading the entire article it is clear that many Christians will be unwittingly convinced that their tithe should not go to the evangelical churches but rather to Herbert W. Armstrong's WORLDWIDE CHURCH OF GOD. What a tragedy!

Quality printing, full color magazines such as THE PLAIN TRUTH and TOMORROW'S WORLD, does and will continue to have great impact in propagating the inventive theology of Herbert W. Armstrong's WORLDWIDE CHURCH of GOD.

GROWING TELEVISION OUTREACH

Along with Armstrong's printed "ministry" is a growing television network of programming which he calls THE WORLD TOMORROW. His son, Garner Ted Armstrong, is the commentator and his program is seen on over 50 television stations weekly.

Anyone who has listened to Garner Ted Armstrong will agree he is a most convincing speaker. He speaks extemporaneously with few notes in both his daily radio and weekly television programs. Usually his only props are a booklet that he offers listeners and a sheaf of news reports. These reports may be on hurricane damage, air pollution, population explosion, crime, or some other evidence that mankind is failing to solve its problems on its own.

Both the radio and television broadcasts are described as "educational" and contain only vague hints of the Armstrong teachings behind them. It is for this reason that a typical reaction of listeners is a combination of fascination and puzzlement.

One Pasadena resident remarked, "He makes so much sense when he's talking...but afterward it's hard to remember exactly what he said."

CONTINUING RADIO IMPACT

Herbert W. Armstrong began his radio broadcasts in 1934. They are now continued by Garner Ted Armstrong. In the last four years his radio outlets have increased from 124 to almost 300 stations. Most of these are daily broadcasts. Armstrong's broadcasts are also heard in Canada, Europe, Asia, the Caribbean and Latin America.

INTERNATIONAL SCOPE

The message of the Worldwide Church of God group reaches around the world. Herbert W. Armstrong himself in the October 1969 issue of THE PLAIN TRUTH estimates that his broadcasts have at least 50 million listeners.

Through advertisements in large space in mass-circulation magazines and newspapers all over the world, with a readership of 150 million, Mr. Armstrong invites people to subscribe to THE PLAIN TRUTH.

In the summer of 1969 Ambassador College had 50 of its students working on an Archaelogical Project in Jerusalem. Along with them were officials of the College and of Armstrong's Church of God.

In a report by the NEW YORK TIMES on Friday, October 10, 1969 the following paragraphs appeared:

> (In the) April, 1969, English issue of THE PLAIN TRUTH (was an article)-written by Herbert W. Armstrong and entitled "Uncovering 3000 years of History!"

> The article described the archeological expedition and asserted that the "throne of David" upon which the future world ruler is to reign is buried "at the very site of our present project." [Jerusalem]

Garner Ted Armstrong, whose programs are telecast over 50 stations in North America.

On the basis of biblical prophecy, Mr. Armstrong concluded that the archeological project had major religious significance. "If a coming world Ruler is to govern the world from the very spot of the ancient throne of David," he said, "the way is certainly being prepared."

If Queen Elizabeth is supposedly sitting on the very Throne of David, one wonders how Mr. Armstrong will reconcile this find with his latest statement above.

The vast empire of Herbert W. Armstrong has grown tremendously since January, 1934 when he started with a small, home-made "magazine" printed on a borrowed mimeograph. Today his organization includes:

THE PLAIN TRUTH
    Magazine   Circulation: 2,550,000

TOMORROW'S WORLD
    Magazine   Circulation: 811,000
(TOMORROW'S WORLD was discontinued in April, 1972)

THE WORLD TOMORROW
    Radio   About 300 stations
    Television   Over 50 stations

AMBASSADOR COLLEGE
                        700 students on EACH of
                        three campuses

CHURCH OF GOD   Approx. 70,000 members
                        167 local churches
                        360 ordained ministers

AMBASSADOR COLLEGE
    PRESS   Printing Plants in 3 locations

But this one thing is important. These figures were accurate at the time of this writing. But, in the words of Herbert W. Armstrong himself as printed in the February, 1970 issue of THE PLAIN TRUTH,

The size and scope of this operation has continued a growth of between 25% and 30% per year. The operation today is huge, having impact on an approximate 150 MILLION people, worldwide!

THE PLAIN TRUTH is printed in many languages. Pictured here from top to bottom are: Dutch, Spanish, German, French and English editions.

HOW OPERATION IS FINANCED

As mentioned earlier Herbert W. Armstrong places a great emphasis in both his printed and radio outlets on TITHING *and* OFFERINGS. It is not unusual for those sold on Armstrong's theology to contribute 20% *or more* of their income *voluntarily* with very little coaxing.

It is easy to become a subscriber to THE PLAIN TRUTH. All one has to do is to write to THE PLAIN TRUTH, Box 111, Pasadena, California 91109 and ask to be placed on their mailing list.

Letters which have the effect of a FUND APPEAL LETTER are sent on a regular basis by Herbert W. Armstrong but their format appears more like a newsletter. The usual letter, 8½x14" long, is four pages in length. The first 3½ pages are like a sermonette. In the November 19, 1969 letter Mr. Armstrong first tells about:

- A. The amazing growth of subscribers to THE PLAIN TRUTH.
- B. A sermon on how THE PLAIN TRUTH helps man understand himself.
- C. A note of praise about Ambassador College Campuses.
- D. An offer to send a booklet titled "FAMINE...Can We Survive?"
- E. An offer to send Garner Ted Armstrong's book on CHILD REARING.
- F. An offer to send a new booklet entitled, "This is *AMBASSADOR COLLEGE.*"
- G. An offer to send a new booklet giving the FACTS on *smoking.*

He then closes with this:

> I'm sure you understand WE HAVE ABSOLUTELY NOTHING TO SELL! This is all a part of the worldwide educational Extension Program of Ambassador College — and these are sent without any cost to you — and there will never be any follow-up with anything to sell. There are no gimmicks in our Program.
>
> I do not want to shove unwanted literature on you, no matter how interesting, vital, valuable I know it to be. Therefore I am simply holding these for you, awaiting your assurance that they will be welcome and are desired. These

Well, from that beginning back in January, 1934, this great worldwide educational program has grown, averaging close to a 30% growth per year. Gradually more and more people, without solicitation from us, VOLUNTEERED to join that little family of Co-Workers who volunteered to become regular contributors. We don't SOLICIT contributors, because we practice the principle of GIVING rather than getting. But we do WELCOME those who WANT to volunteer to have part in a program of GIVING that is changing lives, turning them right-side-up, making them richer, fuller and more abundant.

How is this worldwide enterprise of happiness financed? Wholely by those Co-Workers who have wanted to join with the happiest group I know.

This small contribution of the widow's mites would cause nearly 1,000 people (981 to be exact) to be reached with this great message of hope and inspiration leading to a better and happier life, by these various methods — with an average contribution of only $1.67 per month.

Back in 1902 this widow's 100¢ dollar — or $1.67 per month — could not have reached as effectively anywhere near this number of people. There was no radio and no television then. There was no worldwide organization with the facilities for reaching so many people via such mass media then. And of course it could not be done today, were it not for the fact that more than 100,000 Co-Workers SHARE in this COMMON EFFORT through a Work that has learned how and has the know-how to cut every excess cost, to take advantage of every efficiency method, to make every dollar actually GO FARTHER, I firmly believe, than in any other activity of any kind on earth today.

It is, candidly, one of the amazing success stories of all time. I know of no activity doing so much good to so many people — GIVING OUT to, SHARING WITH, SO MANY PEOPLE, the WAY TO PEACE, HAPPINESS, SUCCESS, ABUNDANT WELL-BEING.

Photographically reproduced from the JUNE-JULY, 1970 issue of The PLAIN TRUTH.

booklets actually and literally are PRICELESS — *you
can't pay for yours!* I know it sounds incredible — you
never heard of any operation like ours before. But I do
hope you'll let me know, in the enclosed self-addressed
return envelope, that you would like to have any or all of
the booklets mentioned.

Anyone who has studied psychology realizes the fine use of
reverse selling in this approach. The very mention of the fact
that (a) you can't pay for yours...it is priceless...coupled with
the idea (b) there are no gimmicks and (c) I'm holding these
for you and (d) let me know in the enclosed self-addressed return envelope if you want them...is enough to send multiple
thousands of Christians and non-Christians alike rushing to
include a check in the mail along with their request. And
they do!

With many born-again people saying, "All those Christian
groups do is beg for money"...is it no wonder they find this
approach not only disarming but appealing? However, if they
were more knowledgeable on the foundations of our Faith they
would not succumb to THE PLAIN TRUTH teachings.

And so the mail pours in to the Pasadena headquarters daily.
So much mail in fact *that it takes 180 men* to open, read, process
and tabulate the daily mail!

They receive as much as a QUARTER MILLION LETTERS
a month! The annual budget is said to be about $55 million. Of
this budget 70% comes from the tithing of church members with
the rest contributed by listeners and other friends. Now, if this
operation grows at the rate of 25% to 30% a year as Mr. Armstrong states...conceivably the budget annually of Herbert W.
Armstrong's operation could grow to

$80 MILLION in 1974
and
$100 MILLION in 1975

Now can you see why Armstrong's WORLDWIDE
CHURCH OF GOD poses one of the greatest, if not the greatest, threat to evangelical Christianity in these last days!

A separate building on the Pasadena Ambassador College campus houses the television facilities. It is filled with the latest telecasting equipment and control panels.

WHO CARRIES ON?

One of the major faults with many Christian organizations is that their success is geared to one prime personality. Look at some of the groups around you. Usually one man is identified as the moving force. And when he dies...that organization slips downhill.

In the case of the WORLDWIDE CHURCH OF GOD, the work is now being transferred to a second personality. Herbert W. Armstrong is now 79. But he has turned over the broadcasting and much of the administrative work to his 42-year old son, Garner Ted Armstrong. And Garner Ted Armstrong is equally as convincing and capable of continuing this work... and is, in fact, already doing so!

Garner Ted Armstrong's responsibilities include:

1. The Church of God
2. Ambassador College
3. The Ambassador College Press
4. The World Tomorrow Radio and Television

As a young man, Garner Ted Armstrong had no intention of affiliating with his father's work. He wanted to become a popular singer. As he himself states: "Then I got tired of slopping around and wasting my money on cigarettes and beer and decided to look for a new kind of life."

Garner Ted Armstrong was removed from the No. 2 spot in late 1971 because of his "personal, emotional problems." He was reinstated to his post as radio and television commentator in the summer of 1972.

Under Garner Ted Armstrong's leadership you can look forward to an aggressive and accelerated growth of this organization.

AMBASSADOR COLLEGE

You will recall this book began with my first impressions of driving down the spacious tree-shaded roads of Pasadena, California towards Ambassador College.

While I am sure Herbert W. Armstrong is proud of all his accomplishments it is my impression that AMBASSADOR COLLEGE is his pride and joy.

In his November 19, 1969 letter sent to over 2 million PLAIN TRUTH subscribers he states:

...readers of The PLAIN TRUTH are beginning to understand some of these BASICS of right knowledge. Lives are being turned right side up. Lives are being enriched. Problems are being solved. They are finding the way to happiness...

Look at the situation on college and university campuses today. Students see no hope for the future. So you see protest, long-haired bearded men, unkempt women. Morals are sinking into the cesspool. Students — entirely too many of them — are experimenting on taking LSD trips and other drugs. You see marches, sit-ins, violence taking over campuses. Student suicides are on the rapid increase — now, next to accidents, the number one cause of student deaths!

Then he talks about Ambassador College:

Then visit one of the three Ambassador College Campuses! There you will see an astonishing *difference!* You'll see clean-cut, alert, animated young men and women who are actually happy! They radiate good cheer. They know how to smile. You'll be surprised at the absence of Hippie-type students. There is no student or faculty revolt. No protest marches — no violence. You'll see students of purpose, who know where they are going and are on their way!

I have visited the Pasadena campus of AMBASSADOR COLLEGE and I must admit the students do radiate good cheer, they are clean-cut...no long hair, and no extreme skirts.

Ambassador College could certainly serve as a model for many evangelical Christian schools who have relaxed their guidelines of dress and decorum.

HOW IT BEGAN

Ambassador College was founded in 1947 "free from the shackles of tradition." It was operated the first four years as an activity of the Church of God which Mr. Armstrong describes as, "...a non-denominational, non-proselyting church."

In the spring of 1952 the college was separately incorporated, and has continued on its own as a college in the Liberal Arts and Sciences ever since.

In the October, 1969 issue of THE PLAIN TRUTH, Mr. Armstrong states:

Although a separate institution from the Church of God, with different functions, there has remained a re-

lationship. I wish to make it clear, however, that neither
this Church nor Ambassador College has any member-
getting program...Further, admission to Ambassador College is not limited to this or any other church membership,
and membership is not a requirement for faculty members.
We employ several who are not.

Ambassador College is non-sectarian, a co-educational
college in the liberal arts, with no discrimination as to
religious faith.

The Ambassador College catalog is a most impressive 62 page
catalog in full color. The photographs of the campus are un-
believable. It is like a "storybook" campus with magnificent
stately buildings, formal Italian Sunken Garden, plaza with
fountain and the most modern student facilities!

There are actually 3 different campuses for AMBASSADOR
COLLEGE.

Pasadena, California

Big Sandy, Texas

St. Albans, England

The Pasadena campus occupies 45 acres and is presently
engaged in a $22 million expansion program.

On each campus the enrollment is purposely limited to 700
students so that individual attention can be given to each one.

At the Pasadena campus students see a $2,500,000 computer,
and a modern television studio which is larger and better
equipped than most television stations. There are major printing plants on each campus. And on the Pasadena campus, there
is a payroll of more than $6,000,000 annually!

At Pasadena and England they see "proud old multi-million-
aire mansions restored to original stateliness, skillfully blended
with award-winning new buildings of classical-modern design."

Herbert W. Armstrong seeks in these Ambassador College
outlets to restore what he calls, "two vital spheres," namely:

1. The Campus Sphere
   Giving them the "right knowledge on *how to live.*"
2. The Home and Family Sphere
   "..education must *begin* in the *home!*"

He apparently is successful for in one of his newsletters he
relates:

New Science Hall which is part of the Loma D. Armstrong Academic Center. Center also includes new Fine Arts Hall, Ambassador Hall, plaza with fountain, and formal Italian Sunken Garden.

One of the first views you see of the Pasadena campus is Ambassador Hall surrounded by beautifully landscaped gardens. It is viewed here from Terrace Drive.

...out of hundreds of marriages of former students who met on an Ambassador Campus, there has, through the years, been only one divorce — and that one contrary to advice of faculty guidance counsellors. To the best of my knowledge all the others are HAPPY marriages.

(November 19, 1969 Letter)

The Texas campus of Ambassador College is Armstrong's division of Agricultural Research. This campus includes a 4000-acre Experimental Farm. This farm provides most of the food for the approximately 1,100 students on the Pasadena and Texas campuses. There is also a 180-acre Experimental Farm on the English campus. Many of Armstrong's articles in THE PLAIN TRUTH deal with experiments to improve agriculture that have been conducted on these farms.

Perhaps its greatest impact is in its extension program. The AMBASSADOR COLLEGE catalog in its closing paragraphs gives some inkling as to its worldwide influence:

Today approximately 150 million *homes* feel the impact of the Ambassador College Extension Program, worldwide. From Ghana to Tasmania, from Okinawa to Argentina, Hawaii to India, one can find Ambassador College publications on anything from History, Archaelogy and Paleontology, Philosophy and Sociology, to modern Criminology and Science — often translated into native tongues.

What an outreach!

"FROM SUCH TURN AWAY"

If only the energies of this organization could be redirected to the true promises of the Word of God! Is it no wonder that people say, "He makes so much sense when he's talking...but afterward it's hard to remember exactly what he said."

When you dig down...through the maze of print...you see here a cult that is most dangerous.

A cult that preaches:

1. Salvation is by faith in Jesus Christ *by which one is enabled to keep the Law.*
2. "... Only those who...have done the works of Christ... shall finally be given immortality."
3. One who is born of God is "merely begotten, spiritually," he is "not yet really BORN." Only those who grow and

50

Ambassador College Press occupies one full block in Pasadena, California. Here is seen one of the large 4-color web-fed magazine presses. Present plans call for 6 such giant presses—3 at Pasadena, one in Sydney, Australia and 2 in England.

develop spiritually "shall finally be given IMMORTAL-ITY..."

4. The soul is not inherently immortal. Only Christ has immortality. The wicked will be annihilated.

5. The condition of all men after death is one of uncon-sciousness. They are totally unconscious until the time of resurrection.

6. The chief beneficiaries of the birthright promise that God made to Abraham have been the modern-day Israelites, the descendants of Ephraim (British Common-wealth) and Manasseh (United States).

7. The *purpose* of your being alive is that you might finally be *born* into the Kingdom of God, when you will actually *be* God...

8. When we are *born of God,* we shall be *spirit*...Jesus Christ was raised from the dead as a spirit...the saints will be resurrected as spirits.

9. ...the blood of Christ does not finally save any man. The death of Christ merely paid the penalty of sin in our stead and wipes the slate clean of *past* sins....

10. For 18½ centuries the Gospel has not been preached. The world was deceived in accepting a false gospel. Today Christ has raised up his work (The World Tomorrow and The Plain Truth) and once again allotted two 19-year time cycles for proclaiming His same Gospel, preparatory to His Second Coming.

11. All those who have died without having had an op-portunity to hear the Gospel (of the World Wide Church of God) will be resurrected and given an opportunity to believe during and after the millennium.

12. That the Holy Spirit is not a person, that all the pro-nouns "He" in John 16:7-14 should be translated "It."

13. That Jesus was not both God and man, when on earth, but was only man. Then at his resurrection Jesus became God again—was "born again"—and He then became a spirit being, and was not actually "flesh and bones." This is contrary to John 2:19-21.

14. That God the Father does not know everything, but is learning, and that though there will be billions of Gods, He will keep learning and remain ahead of all the new Gods to be. This Armstrong doctrine totally ignores Isaiah 43:10, "Before me there was no God formed; nei-ther shall there be after me." And Isaiah 44:6, "I am the first, and I am the last; and beside me there is no God."

And to sum it up (15)...as Mr. Armstrong has stated:

"...no other work on earth is proclaiming this true Gospel of Christ to the whole world."

ANOTHER NEIGHBOR?

If Christians are going to read THE PLAIN TRUTH and listen to THE WORLD OF TOMORROW they should be made aware they are stepping on dangerous ground.

If through their tithes and offerings they give to this organization, they should be made aware what cult pronouncements they are supporting...in direct contradiction to the Word of God.

And it all started when Herbert W. Armstrong was 34 years of age...visiting his parents in Salem, Oregon. A neighbor of the Armstrong parents was an "evangelist" for a misdirected cause. But she caught the ear of Herbert Armstrong's wife, Loma. And from that day sprang a message that is now heard around the world!

Perhaps I'm a dreamer. As I said before, humanly speaking, I admire the aggressive business ability of Herbert W. Armstrong. We need this zealousness as Christians.

Perhaps...someday...another neighbor, rooted in the Word of God, will point THE WAY to Herbert Armstrong or his son, Garner Ted. And then, perhaps, if God wills, this voice of Confusion, will become a powerful modern day Paul.

Perhaps...if you and I pray...perhaps...another neighbor will change the course of history!

Why the vast difference between animal brain and

HUMAN MIND?

ADVANCE STUDIES in the new science of Brain Research have made significant progress toward unlocking the ultimate secrets of the vast superiority of the human MIND over animal brain.

Whatever the amazing complexity of the human brain, the same is true of animal brain — in only slightly lesser degree, both quantitatively and qualitatively.

Yet man has amazing intellectual powers almost totally absent from highest animal brains — seemingly out of all proportion to the slight difference in quantity and quality of brain content.

How explain these awesome intellectual powers of man?

. . . intellectual, ethical, moral consciousness
. . . ability to THINK and reason creatively
. . . comprehension of technological processes
. . . appreciation of art, literature, music
. . . awareness of facts, values and principles
. . . self-consciousness, capacity for possessing knowledge, understanding and wisdom foreign to animal brain.

WHY this transcendent difference?

Beginning with the January 1972 number, *The PLAIN TRUTH* magazine will begin publication of a new, remarkable series of articles on this most vital subject. Request your three-month trial subscription — NO CHARGE.

Already–Paid 3–month TRIAL SUBSCRIPTION

You've never read a magazine like the PLAIN TRUTH. Written in a fast-moving, scintillating, easy-to-understand, PLAIN TRUTH style utterly unique among leading magazines. A magazine of quality, tone and character — profusely illustrated, full color. None is like it!

The PLAIN TRUTH magazine is published monthly as part of the Ambassador College worldwide educational program. Circulation over 2,000,000 — readership over 6,000,000 worldwide. Our editors bring you the BIG ISSUES — world news, science, social, family and personal problems, with thoroughly researched ANSWERS that make sense! And without charge — an educational service to the public. Try the PLAIN TRUTH magazine for three months. We think you'll be surprised and delighted.

The Plain Truth
a magazine of understanding

Write: Ambassador College Press, Box 111, Pasadena, Calif. 91109

AMBASSADOR COLLEGE PRESS, P.O. Box 111, Pasadena, Calif. 91109

Please send me ALREADY-PAID a three-month trial subscription to *The PLAIN TRUTH*, starting with the January 1972 number.

Mr.
Mrs.
Miss _____

Address _____

_____

Zip _____ 100-4x1

No Cost – No Obligation

The above advertisement appeared in many secular publications including LIFE magazine and READER'S DIGEST.

53882

Garner Ted Armstrong, Where Are You?

Until last fall, lean, gray-templed Garner Ted Armstrong was the quintessential religious soft-sell artist. His program called *The World Tomorrow* was carried on some 400 radio and 99 TV stations. His slick, free monthly called *The Plain Truth* went to 2,100,-000 subscribers. To the millions of Americans who followed him, Garner Ted dispensed glib solutions to such problems as drugs, crime, broken marriages and delinquent children—all implicitly in the name of the Worldwide Church of God. This is a stern, bizarre sect founded in 1934 as the Radio Church of God by Garner Ted's father Herbert W. Armstrong, a Quaker-born ad salesman turned preacher, and still ruled by the elder Armstrong from headquarters in Pasadena, Calif. Garner Ted, 42, was the heir apparent not only to the W.C.G. but also to a church-run institution called Ambassador College: three campuses (in Pasadena; Big Sandy, Texas; and St. Albans, England) where the buildings are expensive and the tuition cheap, the boys' sideburns high and the girls' skirts low.

Then, last October, Garner Ted was suddenly relieved of duties as executive vice president of the church and vice chancellor of Ambassador College. Later his name was expunged from the masthead of *The Plain Truth*. His radio programs were replaced by ten-year-old tapes made by his father.

Bonds of Satan. At first, Herbert told [...] members that Garner Ted

will fight the battle of Armageddon with the victor. At first, Herbert Armstrong predicted the beginning of the end for the late 1930s. The most recent Apocalypse was due on Jan. 7, 1972.

In other departures from traditional Christianity, Armstrong and his faithful worship on Saturday, not Sunday; they observe kosher laws set forth in the Old Testament. They celebrate Passover but not Christmas or Easter. They deny the Trinity. But they believe steadfastly in the tithe—so much so that each member is expected to set aside three tithes, [...] tenths of his gross income. One-tenth

THE NEW YORK TIMES, SUNDAY, MAY 7, 1972

Radio Preacher Is Ousted by Father

Special to The New York Times

PASADENA, Calif. May 6—Garner Ted Armstrong, nationally known radio preacher, has been ousted as second in command of his father's monolithic Worldwide Church of God.

He has been replaced "indefinitely" on the daily broadcast "World Tomorrow," as vice chancellor of Ambassador College here and as executive editor of the two-million circulation magazine The Plain Truth.

According to his father, Herbert W. Armstrong, founder-president of the fundamentalist body, Garner Ted is on "indefinite leave" because of "personal and emotional problems."

In a letter from the elder Mr. Armstrong to all congregations of the 70,000-member sect, the son was said to be "in the bonds of Satan."

Hints of a falling-out between father and son came to light last October. Directors of the church and Ambassador College say [...] choice" but [...] year-old son [...] spot.

Les Stocke [...] director at th [...] maculately k [...] pus here, sai [...] agreed to st [...] took a leave [...] fall.

Attempt [...]

Herbert A [...] ered by som [...] prophet, [...] control of [...] Church of G [...] Saturday as [...] last week [...] statement [...] from an ex [...] Mr. Armstro [...]

tude and conduct—to our great dismay—demonstrated to board members, ministers and myself that the process of repentance was not yet complete."

A confidential letter was sent to each of the 250 pastors of the church in February. It said that Garner Ted was "in the bonds of Satan."

One source said that the son had written his father confessing "I have sinned against my wife, the children and the church."

Neither of the Armstrongs nor Ambassador College spokesmen have elaborated on the alleged confession. Herbert Armstrong, a former public relations man, did say, however, that the breach "does not involve any personal conflict or doctrinal dispute between my son and myself."

Mr. Stocker, the public relations director, confirmed that the expression "in the bonds of Satan" had been used in the letter to pastors, but, he said,

the son on the daily "World of Tomorrow" broadcast heard on 300 stations worldwide. Lately, most of the programs have been transcribed live from Herbert Armstrong messages.

Garner Ted's half-hour television show, has been dropped by about 50 stations, but Re-runs of the World's documentaries are televised sporadically, according to Mr. Stocker.

New names replace Garner Ted's on the mastheads in the two slick, full-color magazines produced here.

Herman L. Hoeh is now executive editor of The Plain Truth, a free monthly sent to two-million radio listeners, and David Jon Hill is now managing editor of Ambassador College's Tomorrow's World, sent free to about 800,000 subscribers.

Albert J. Portune has been assigned Mr. Armstrong's No. 2 post at the campus here.

The college has 700 students here, 550 at a Big Sandy, Texas,

'Repentant' Returns to Air

PASADENA, Calif. — Garner Ted Armstrong is back at his post as radio and television commentator for the Worldwide Church of God and Ambassador College, both headquartered here.

With his father, Herbert W. Armstrong, standing at his side, the church leader said his private life is no one else's

business and that his public life is more than ever dedicated to God.

The senior Armstrong, founder of the church and college, said he permitted his son to return last month after suspension last winter for disciplinary reasons.

He said his son's repentance, a condition of return from several months of exile in Colorado, is "full and permanent, otherwise he wouldn't be here."

The two men met with a Pasadena newsman as Garner Ted prepared a 30-minute television segment on "Proof of God."

Garner Ted's suspension for undisclosed reasons rocked the 75,000 member religious group.

[...] questioned whether the church had the proper presence of the Holy Spirit.

Whatever the cause of Garner Ted's

GARNER TED ARMSTRONG

HERBERT ARMSTRONG AT PASADENA CAMPUS

The above newspaper clippings and letter from Herbert W. Armstrong convey in part the story of Garner Ted Armstrong brief departure from his father's doctrine and the Worldwide Church of God.

8 300

TE DUE